The Depression Cure Formula:

7- Steps To Beat Depression Naturally Now

Table of Contents

Introduction

Depression affects 1 in 10 people all over the US. It's one of the most common of mental illnesses and one of the easiest to treat.

According to CDC (Centers for Disease Control and Prevention) the most likely of people to suffer with depression are:

- ➢ People 45 – 64 years of age
- ➢ Women
- ➢ People who are unable to work or are unemployed
- ➢ Been previously married
- ➢ People without health insurance coverage

See stats below:

	N#	Major depression %	Other depression %	Any depression %
Total	235,067	4.1	5.1	9.1
Age group:				
• 18-24	9,944	3.7	7.3	11.1
• 25-34	27.086	4.2	5.1	9.3
• 35-44	39.440	4.3	4.4	8.7
• 45-64	97.642	4.9	4.7	9.6
• 65+	59.246	2.1	4.8	6.9
Gender:				
• Male	89.842	3.3	4.8	8.0
• Female	145.225	4.8	5.3	10.2
Marital Status:				
• Married	133.642	2.7	3.9	6.6
• Previously Married	65.789	7.7	6.9	14.6
• Never Married	34.850	5.0	6.7	11.8
Healthcare plan:				
• Yes	208.323	3.6	4.5	8.0
• No	26.265	7.0	8.2	15.2
Employment Status:				
• Employed	133.951	2.4	4.1	6.6
• Unemployed	8.991	11.4	10.1	21.5
• Retired	55.172	2.1	4.3	6.4
• Unable to work	13.054	25.9	13.5	39.3
• Homemaker or student	23.447	3.9	5.5	9.3

So even if we take what this study says verbatim then the majorities suffering with depression are those unemployed with no health insurance, so going down the "normal" routes of seeking out a psychiatric professional is out of the question.

The usual cost for a psychologist is $120 to $180 per 50-minute session. Some even charge a $250 first time evaluation fee!

Even for those that do have health insurance packages, it'll only pay for so many sessions before you have to start paying for it yourself. Most insurance companies pay for the first 10 sessions and then after that you're on your own. Some will pay a quarter of what the psychologist charges per hour and the rest you have to pay.

So what are the alternatives?

You could go to your family doctor and get prescribed anti-depressants. Let's take a look at some of them.

The most commonly prescribed anti-depressants are:

- Prozac
- Luvox
- Zoloft
- Paxil
- Lexapro

These act on a chemical in the brain called serotonin. However like all anti-depressants the above five I've listed increase suicidal thoughts and behaviors as well as increasing hostility, agitation and anxiety.

They also have some horrible side effects such as:

- Nausea
- Insomnia
- Headaches
- Decreased sexual desires
- Sweating
- Tremors
- Weight loss or gain
- Dry mouth
- Diarrhea or constipation
- Dizziness
- Drowsiness and fatigue

Just what you need when you are suffering with depression. However there are other alternatives that are cost effective with zero side effects. Lets take a look at "7 Rapid Step Program to Beating Depression!"

Step 1 – Eating Healthily

Ok, so we hear this everywhere right? Every thing that you have wrong with you in this day and age revolves around what you eat. Now I'm no health freak and I love, beer, pizza, burgers, chocolate and all the stuff I'm NOT supposed to eat. However there has to be something in what the "gotta eat healthy" crowds are saying so lets take a look.

We all need food to stay alive, fit and healthy. Vitamins and minerals found in the foods that we eat effect our bodies in different ways. However the two most common jobs of our food is to replenish cells and the vital organs within our bodies and to control what hormones we produce and when.

To eat healthy is not just a case of what you eat but how you eat it. What you chose to put into your bodies can help you reduce the risk of illnesses such as:

- Heart disease
- Cancer
- Diabetes
- Help against depression!

Read the last bullet point again. The food that we eat can help against depression!

Why? Certain foods boost your energy levels; sharpen your memory and helps to lift your mood.

Lets take a look at these "super mood lifting" vitamins and minerals, how they affect you and what foods are they in.

1. Zinc

Low Zinc levels are said to contribute to depression. A study was conducted on 48 depressed patients and it found that the lower the Zinc levels the deeper the depression[1].

So what does Zinc do for us? Zinc is a mineral that is vital for growth and development and plays a major role in our immune responses, brain functions and the ability to reproduce. The recommended daily allowance for men is 11mg and 9mg for women.

Foods containing Zinc are:

- Oysters
- Animal livers
- Sesame seeds
- Beef
- Lamb
- Peanuts
- Dark chocolate
- Cheddar Cheese
- Kidney Beans

2. Iron

Iron is essential for neurological functions and development. If you have low levels of Iron in your body then it can lead to tiredness, irritability, difficulty in concentrating and depression.

The recommended daily intake of iron for men is 8mg and 18mg for women.

Foods containing Iron are:

---

[1] http://www.ncbi.nlm.nih.gov/pubmed/8071476

- Red meat
- Dried fruits
- Artichokes
- Egg yolks
- Beans and lentils
- Oatmeal
- Spinach
- Whole wheat bread
- Cereals

3. Vitamin C

Our bodies are unable to make vitamin C so we need to get from the foods that we eat. Vitamin C is required for the production of protein collagen, which we have in our skin and bones. It also supports our bodies' tissues and helps us heal wounds as well as assisting in our biochemical reactions, hence why vitamin C is essential when you are suffering with depression.

The recommended daily intake is 90mg for men and 75mg for women.

Foods containing vitamin C are:

- Red/Green chili peppers
- Guavas
- Dark leafy greens
- Oranges
- Kiwi
- Broccoli
- Cauliflower
- Strawberries
- Blueberries

Meat also has vitamin C however the cooking process kills the vitamin.

4. Omega 3 fatty acids

Omega-3 fatty acids reduces inflammation and can help lower risk of chronic diseases such as heart disease, cancer, and arthritis. Omega-3 fatty acids are highly concentrated in the brain and are important for cognitive (brain memory and performance) and behavioral function.

Symptoms of omega-3 fatty acid deficiency include fatigue, poor memory, dry skin, heart problems, mood swings or depression, and poor circulation.

The recommended daily intake of Omega 3 is 1.6g or men and 1.1g for women.

Foods containing Omega 3 fatty acids are:

- Salmon
- Tuna
- Walnuts
- Flax cereal
- Sardines
- Most other oily fish

5. Calcium

Calcium is necessary for our physical and mental health. Most of our calcium intake goes to our bones and teeth but the remaining goes to helping the release of neurotransmitters, which serve as messengers between cells within the nervous system.

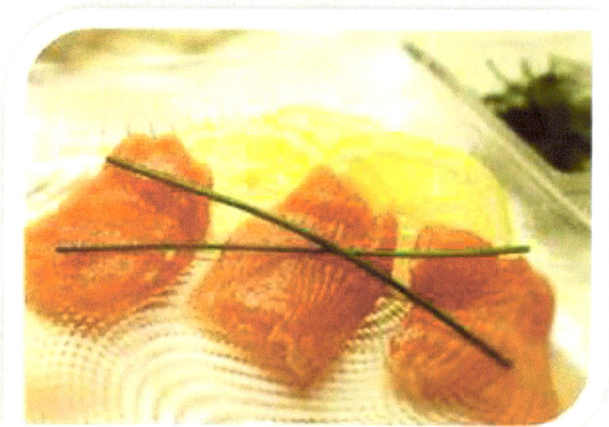

Long-term calcium deficiency can lead to nerve sensitivity, twitching muscles, brittle nails, palpitations, mood and behavior problems such as irritability, anxiety, depression, and insomnia.

The recommended daily intake of calcium is 1000mg for men and 1000mg for women.

Foods containing Calcium are:

- Milk
- Yoghurt
- Cheese
- Broccoli
- Red kidney beans
- Baked beans
- Almonds
- Hazelnuts
- Oranges
- Figs
- Salmon

6. Vitamin B-12

Vitamin B-12 and other B vitamins
play a role in producing brain
chemicals that affect mood and other brain functions. Low levels of B-12 and
other B vitamins such as vitamin B-6 and folate may be linked to depression.

The recommended daily intake of vitamin B12 is 2.4 mcg for men and 2.4mcg
for women.

Foods containing Vitamin B12 are:

- Beef liver
- Clams
- Trout
- Salmon
- Haddock
- Plain yogurt
- Eggs
- Cured Ham
- Chicken

So as you can see the foods that we put into our bodies really do help towards
beating depression. Just making simple changes in our diet can help and so
can eating chocolate ☺ it's well known for its feel good properties.

Eating healthy doesn't have to be bland and boring and remember that you can eat anything as long as it's in moderation but by just eating some of the foods I've mentioned above can really help lift your mood. Below are some illustrations by Harvard School of Public Health who says what we should be having in our diet and what should go onto our plates to make us feel great.

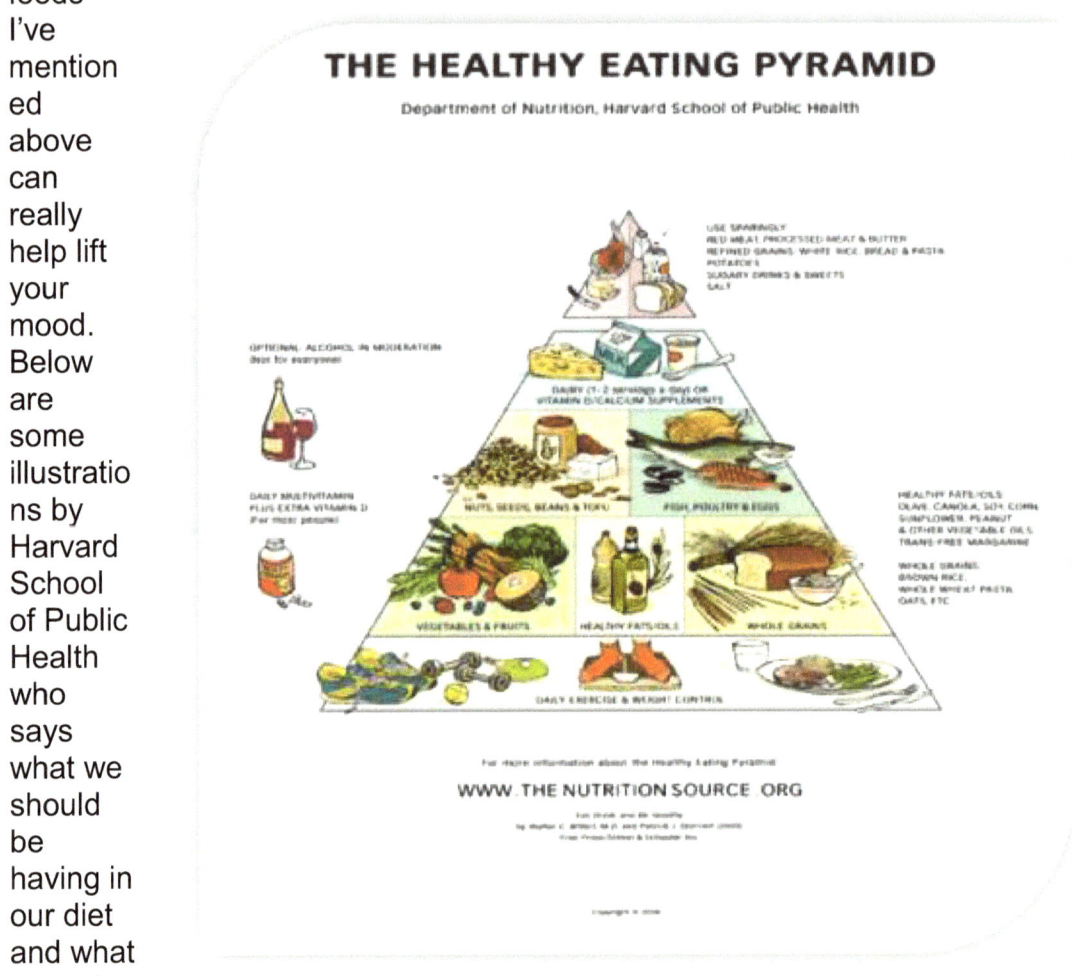

Step 2 – Get More Exercise

Your next step in "7 Rapid Step Program to Beating Depression" runs hand in hand with the healthy eating we covered in the last step.

Exercising for at least 30 minutes a day, four to five times a week doesn't just make you look great but makes you feel great too.

Regular exercise can really help you to reduce your stress levels, anxiety and depression. When you exercise your brain releases endorphins.

Endorphins are naturally produced by your body and they:

- Control persistent pain
- Control cravings (including addictive ones)
- Controls feelings of stress and frustration
- Regulates the production of the growth and sex hormones ☺

It's like a legal way of getting high and you produce it when you exercise. According to the Mayo Clinic[2] regular physical activity has 7 benefits:

1. It controls your weight

Many people get depressed because of their weight or they gain weight because of their depression. Either way if you do the first step I told you about combined with exercise then surely your going to look better which is going to make you feel better about yourself if you lose the weight.

---

[2] http://www.mayoclinic.com/health/exercise/HQ01676

2. It combats health conditions and diseases

Even if you aren't over weight exercise helps control things such as strokes, heart disease, diabetes and depression.

3. It improves your mood

Even a 30-minute walk can help you blow of some steam and reduce stress levels.

4. It boosts energy levels

One of the side effects of depression is feeling fatigued and low energy levels. Exercise and physical activities delivers oxygen and nutrients to your tissues, which helps you work more efficiently and gives you more energy to go about your daily routines.

5. It helps you sleep better

Another known side effect of depression can be that you can't sleep. You feel tired all day but when you actually get to bed your mind will not shut off. If this is for a prolonged period then you are actually depressed.

As long as you don't exercise too close to bedtime then it can help you fall asleep faster and have a deeper sleep

6. Helps with your sex life ☺

Regular physical activity can lead to enhanced arousal for women and men are said to suffer less with erectile dysfunction.

7. It can be fun!

Apparently (only joking) if your one of those that thinks a 1-hour session at the gym doesn't sound fun to you then you're not alone. But sweating your behind off in a gym for one hour isn't the only form of exercise out there.

So what great and fun exercises can we do?

Try not to look at exercise as exercise but more about having fun. You don't have to do these on your own but with a family member or with friends. Here's a great list of fun, feel good exercises that you can combine to make your four to five times a week.

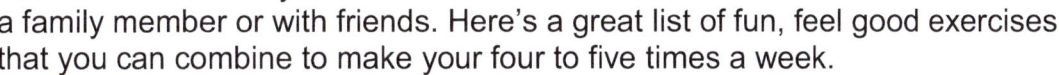

- Ballet
- Baseball
- Boxing
- Dancing
- Football
- Golf
- Hiking
- Horse riding
- Ice skating
- Paint balling
- Roller blading
- Swimming
- Tennis
- Walking
- Wii gaming
- Yoga

See and not a sweaty gym in sight!

Step 3 – Relax

Ok so now your eating right and doing some exercise it's now time to relax! When I mean relax I don't mean reading a book or watching TV. This isn't the type of relaxation that I'm talking about; I'm talking about proper relaxation techniques.

We are told many times that we need to relax more but yet no one really tells us how we can relax.

What's so beneficial about relaxing?

Depression and chronic stress has been linked together by many research physiologists which suggests that depression is partly caused by a high level of anxiety. It's because of this that a part of your nervous system triggers the fight/flight response.

One of the responses of fight/flight is to cause the muscles in our bodies to become tense. This is ok when it's needed to deal with a threat however in the long term due to excessive stress or anxiety it can cause chronic muscle tension.

This results in pain and can cause headaches, back and neck pain. So what we need to do is turn off your fight/flight response and trigger the relaxation response. Both responses are triggered in the hypothalamus gland which means that relaxation techniques has to work because we can't be tense and relaxed at the same time.

So if we can get our fight\flight responses under control then we can reduce our depression.

What happens to our bodies when we are in the fight/flight response?

- Our anxiety levels increase

- Our body prepares for fight or flight
- Our blood pressure increases
- We sweat more
- Our pulse rates increase
- Our muscle tension increases
- Our blood flow to our muscles increases
- Our breathing increases
- Our brains goes into hyperactivity

So what happens to our bodies when we are in a relaxed state? Obviously the opposite happens.

- Our anxiety levels decrease
- Our body prepares for rest
- Our blood pressure decreases
- Our pulse rates return to normal
- Our muscles relax
- Our blood flow to our muscles normalizes
- Our breathing stabilizes
- Our brain is relaxed

So how do we get to this state? There are a number of techniques to can try to get your body to relax.

- Acupuncture
- Breathing exercises
- Guided Imagery
- Massage
- Meditation
- Progressive muscle relaxation
- Yoga

Lets take a look at a few of these.

1. Breathing Exercises

Deep breathing techniques are very simple to do yet very effective.

<u>Try the following for 2-3 minutes:</u>

- Breathe slowly and deeply in through your nose, and out through your mouth in a steady rhythm.
- Try to make your breath out twice as long as your breath in. To do this you may find it helpful to count slowly "one, two" as you breathe in, and "one, two, three, four" as you breathe out.
- Try to relax your shoulders and upper chest muscles when you breathe. With each breath out, consciously try to relax those muscles until you are mainly using your diaphragm to breathe.

2. Guided Imagery

This technique is a bit like daydreaming and involves using positive and happy images. These things can be anything from being in a meadow on a beautiful warm, sunny day surrounded by pretty flowers or on a secluded beach listening to the waves crashing on the beach or a remote waterfall etc.

For the technique to really work to need to use all of your scenes such as touch, taste, smell and sight.

Here's an example of how you would do it.

- Get into a comfortable position this can either be reclining in an armchair or lying on the couch.

- Do the above breathing technique and imagine that you are breathing in inner peace and breathing out stress.

- When you are feeling calm and relaxed then you can start to imagine

Example:

"Imagine that you are sitting in that beautiful meadow on a warm and sunny day. As you breathe in you can smell the sweet smell of the flowers that surround you. You can hear the rustling of the trees from the light breeze that's just wafted over your warm skin. You open your eyes and take a look around you. You reach out and touch the delicate petal of a flower floating next to you."

Do you get the idea? The place or what you do there can be anything that makes you feel happy, calm and relaxed. It can be like taking a mini vacation.

You can do this for a long as you like and as many times as you like as long as you have peace and quite and the time to do it. But try it at least once a week.

3. Progressive muscle relaxation

A guy called Dr. Edmund Jacobson over 50 years ago developed progressive muscle relaxation. It's used to achieve a deep state of relaxation.

He realized that muscles could be relaxed by tensing the muscle first. By first tensing various muscle groups and then relaxing them brings about a sense of deep relaxation.

You need to really do this technique for 20 minutes a day, preferably twice a day but you can stick to doing it the once if you want to. You need to find a quite, calm and peaceful place. Try to do it on an empty stomach as apparently a full stomach detracts from deep relaxation. Try not to wear tight fitting clothes either.

How it works?

Progressive muscle relaxation involves tensing and then relaxing 16 different muscle groups for about 10 seconds and then releasing them. You need to put all your attention on that muscle group while you are doing the tensing and relaxing bit.

- **Hands** – Clench your fists for 10 seconds and the relax it and outstretch the fingers. Wait and put all of your attention on the feelings in your hands for the next 10 to 15 seconds.
- **Biceps and triceps** – Tense the muscles for 10 seconds and then let your muscles relax and drop your arms by your side. While tensing however makes sure that you don't clench you fist. Your hands need to be loose. Again wait and put all of your attention on the feelings in your arms for the next 10 to 15 seconds.
- **Shoulders** – Pull them back for 10 seconds and then relax them. Then push them forward for 10 seconds then relax them. Remember that on EVERY muscle group you need to wait to 10 to 15 seconds before moving on to the next muscle group and all the time observe the feelings within that muscle.
- **Neck** – Bring your head forward so that your chin is touching your chest. Do not put your head backwards as it cold cause an injury.
- **Head** – Turn this to the left, hold for 10 seconds and then turn it to the right
- **Mouth** – Open your mouth as wide as possible for 10 seconds then relax. Then tighten the lips together and then relax
- **Tongue** – With you mouth open pull out your tongue as far as possible, relax then bring it to the back of your throat and then relax
- **Tongue** – Dig your tongue into the roof of your mouth, relax and then push it to the bottom and then relax. Remember the hold for 10 seconds and then wait for 10 to 15 seconds, well it applies to everyone ok?
- **Eyes** – Open your eyes as wide as possible and then relax them. Then scrunch them as tight as possible and then relax them.
- **Breathing** – Take a deep a breath as possible, then take a little more, then let it out. Breath normally for 15 seconds then breath out until your lungs is empty and then a little more. Then breath normally for 15 seconds.
- **Back** – With your shoulders resting on the back of a chair push out your body until your back is arched. If you suffer with back problems then you might want to give this one a miss until you have spoken with your doctor.
- **Butt** – Clench your butt cheeks, slightly raising your pelvis off the chair. Then relax. Then push your butt down in the chair then relax.

- **Thighs** – Extend your legs and raise them about six inches off the floor but don't use your stomach muscles. Then relax. Then dig your heels into the floor and relax
- **Stomach** – Pull in the stomach as far as possible and then relax. Push out the stomach or tense it as if you were going to get a punch, then relax.
- **Calves and feet** – Point your toes but without raising your legs, then relax. Then pull your feet up to your shin and then relax.
- **Toes** – With your legs relaxed push your toes into the floor and then relax. Then pull up your toes and then relax.

Step 4 – Connect With Others

When you are feeling depressed it can be very easy to stop seeing people. You want to seclude yourself from others and hide away spending a lot of time by yourself. However you need to stop yourself from doing this.

Since most people can't afford to talk to a professional then you need to get support from somewhere else.

The most obvious choice is a family member. This doesn't have to be someone too close to you such as your partner or parents but it could be an aunt or an uncle. Someone you feel close enough to open up to him or her about how you are feeling or what you are going through.

You might want to talk to a friend. You never know, they may have at some point in their life suffered the same as what you are suffering with now. Even if you don't want to open up to them make sure that you still continue to see them.

Try to arrange it so that you do something social with them on a weekly or fortnightly event. This doesn't have to cost you the earth like going out for a meal together but just going out for a coffee and having a chat about something nice. Or go window-shopping or go play one of the sports mentioned in the exercise step earlier on in this guide.

If you don't have friends or a family member that you can connect with then you can always try the Internet. There are lots of forums out there for people to connect together that cater for depression and depressed people. Just listening or reading in this case, to what others are going through or have gone through is beneficial.

You never know you might even make some new friends. Even if you don't want to get in touch with other people suffering with depression, you can still use the Internet to make new friends.

There are plenty of websites out there that you can join, most of them are free to join and you can meet people from all over the world. It's a bit like having a pen pal ☺

If you want to make friends in the "real" world then why don't you attend a group or a class in a particular subject or hobby? If you aren't good with meeting new people then you can take a social skills class and this will help you to improve your communication skills.

Not only will you meet new people that have similar interests to you but it will also help keep you mind off things and give you something to look forward to. It also gets you out of the house.

Similarly you can find groups that are for depression sufferers. You can usually find these by visiting your local health care center or community center. Most of these groups are free because volunteers run them. Some may charge you a small fee but they won't be expensive.

The whole point about this step is to stop you from isolating yourself and getting you out there sharing your life and your experiences with other. This step alone can help towards beating depression.

Go on get yourself out there!

Step 5 – Stay Away From Self-Medicating

Something that people suffering with depression tend to do a lot of is self-medicate themselves.

Self-medicating could be anything from buying anti-depressants over the Internet rather than getting them prescribed for you by a professional, excessive drinking of alcohol or substance abuse.

- **Getting anti-depressants from over the Internet**

I actually can't believe that you can buy anti-depressants over the Internet but you can! I'm not saying that anti-depressants don't play an important role in dealing and beating depression but these things have some very nasty side

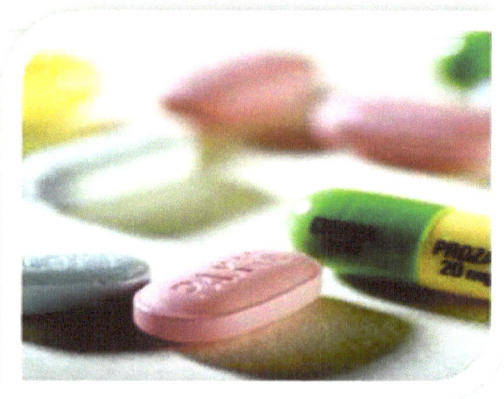

effects and only your doctor can really know what to prescribe you.

If you go down the anti-depressant route it's extremely important that you only get them prescribed to you by a proper professional.

Not all anti-depressants work for all people so it's extremely important that you get the right anti-depression at the right dose.

Get this wrong and you could suffer some very real and very painful consequences. DON'T GET THEM FROM THE INTERNET! Go to your doctor and get them via the proper channels.

- **Alcohol**

It's a known fact that alcoholism can grip you when you are at your lowest point. Depression, stress and anxiety can result in us using something as a coping mechanism.

Drinking alcohol to make you feel better is the worst thing that you can do. It can be tempting to have a glass of wine or two or a nice ice cold beer with friends when you are feeling down and low but alcohol can actually make depression worse.

Alcohol reduces the serotonin in our brains and as we know it's serotonin that makes us feel better and happy. Alcohol is a depressant in itself. So if you are drinking too much then you need to try to stop because you will feel better for it. After a couple of weeks not drinking you will probably find that your moods will feel lighter.

- ### Substance Abuse

As well as using alcohol to make us feel better some people turn to drugs (not anti-depressants) to make themselves feel better.

The kind of drugs I'm taking about are things such as marijuana, heroin, and crystal meth, cocaine and ecstasy.

These types of drugs shouldn't be taken anyway let alone if you have depression. It can be easy to get yourself in a vicious cycle. Substance abuse leads to depression and depression leads to substance abuse.

Drugs make people feel better on the surface because they control our emotions. Certain drugs control certain chemicals in our brain. Because of this is can be hard to treat depression while you are still on drugs. So if you are then you need to get help with your substance abuse before you can deal with your depression.

Depending on the drug that you are taking will depend on whether you can just stop taking them or not. If you are on a highly addictive drug then you are going to need some serious help to get yourself off them because the withdrawal effects are massive.

So what drugs do what to the chemicals in your brain?

- Heroin
- Morphine
- Codeine
- Pethidine
- Methadone

These are powerful painkillers when using these to excess produces feelings of euphoria. They are also highly addictive. Heavy or long term abuse of these drugs can lead to ill health.

- Marijuana

The effects of marijuana depend on the mood that the person is in when they take it. Generally it exaggerates the pre existing mood, so if you are feeling down when you take it then you are going to feel even worse.

- Cocaine

This is a stimulant but when it starts to wear off people tend to "come down" where they feel low, have no energy, and are fatigued and anxious. Continued use makes people have suicidal thoughts and paranoia.

Step 6 – Adopt a Positive Thinking Attitude

When you are depressed you think negative thoughts so to beat depression you need to change those negative thoughts and think of positive ones.

I want to provide you with some positive quotes to make you feel uplifted.

"We are what we think. All that we are arises with our thoughts. With our thoughts, we make our world"
Buddha

"A man is but the product of his thoughts. What he thinks he becomes"
Mahatma Gandhi

"Become a possibilitarian. No matter how dark things seem to be or actually are, raise your sights and see possibilities - always see them, for they're always there"
Norman Vincent Peale

"If you don't like something change it; if you can't change it, change the way you think about it"
Mary Engelbreit

"I don't think of all the misery but of the beauty that still remains"
Anne Frank

"Consult not your fears but your hopes and your dreams. Think not about your frustrations, but about your unfulfilled potential. Concern yourself not with what you tried and failed in, but with what it is still possible for you to do."
Pope John XXIII

"Once you replace negative thoughts with positive ones, you'll start having positive results."
Willie Nelson

"Happiness is an attitude. We either make ourselves miserable, or happy and strong. The amount of work is the same."
Francesca Reigle

Write these out on post it notes and stick them all over your house ☺ read them whenever you start to think negative thoughts.

Try to follow these thought patterns and you should start to feel better.

- Believe that you are special and that you deserve the best in life

- Rather than focusing on your failures or what you haven't achieved look at all the good things that you have accomplished and what you have still yet to achieve
- Think about all the good things in life what you already have. Don't think about the things that you don't have.
- Surround yourself with loving, caring, happy people and get rid of the negative people that drag you down.

Step 7 - Keep A Journal

Your final step to beating depression is keeping a journal. You might be thinking that journals are for teenage girls to write about their latest crush or the girl that they hate at school etc. but that's not the case.

Keeping a journal helps with depression in a number of ways.

1. To get your thoughts and emotions out of your head and on to paper.

Well it doesn't have to be on paper it can be done using your computer but I think writing it in a book works better.

This is because you can do it at the end of the day. This helps you to relax ready for sleep, whereas the computer may stimulate your brain, which isn't good when you are trying to go to sleep.

Getting your thoughts and emotions out of your head helps you to release that pent up energy, thoughts, emotions and feelings that you have locked deep inside yourself. As a depressive you know that keeping these emotions within you doesn't help your depression get better.

2. It shows your progress or lack of it.

Sometimes, we look back on the weeks and months and wonder what actually happened. The great thing about keeping a journal is you can see how far that you have come or how far you still need to go. This can help with confidence and self-esteem when you see the kind of steps that you have made or are making. It also gives you a benchmark to reach to if you are lacking progress.

If you aren't making as much progress as you would like, don't beat yourself up about it. Keeping a journal is not supposed to be a negative experience it's supposed to be a positive one so treat it that way. If you haven't progressed as far as you would have liked, look back over the things that you have wrote in your journal and take comfort in the things that you have accomplished up to date. Then think about how you are going to move forward.

3. Makes you take a good look at yourself.

Because of the negative thoughts and emotions that you are feel impacts on your depression and essentially makes it worse. When you look back over what you have wrote in the past, you would be able to spot all of your negativity.

Being able to see these and recognize them you will then be able to change them because you'll be able to spot a pattern forming of where and when you feel them. This will help you to change the way that you look at those situations when you face them again.

4. Gives you a platform to be yourself.

Sometimes it can be very hard to talk to people about what you are feeling especially if you feel the same things on a regular basis such as dread, anxiety and panic. You get a feeling that the person with whom you confide in must say to themselves "oh get a grip, we're back on the same subject of feeling low again" So you can be reluctant at times to keep talking about your problems.

Well a journal is like having that friend except it never gets bored of listening to the same problems over and over again. It gives you the space and the platform to just vent out your anger, frustrations, and pent up emotions.

5. Helps you to realize that things aren't that bad.

If you suffer from panic attacks or anxiousness with your depression then writing your thoughts and feelings down at the time that they occur makes you realize that your panic attacks for example aren't going to result in anything serious happening to you.

Most people that suffer with panic attacks and over anxiousness feel that they are going to die. Their chests tighten and they feel short of breath, they think they are going to faint. However I'm not aware of any death related to having a panic attack.

When you are in the grips of one write down your sensations and feelings such as tightened chest, racing heart, shortness of breath. Also note where you are and what started them off. Writing them at the moment they are happening to you can help the panic attack finish more quickly. After your anxious period has finished look back at those thoughts and feeling and note down the actually effects they had on you for example:

- Racing heart – did I pass out or die? No I'm still here!
- Tightened Chest – did I stop breathing? No I'm still here!

Get the picture? After a while you'll come to realize that even if your chest tightens or you get shortness of breathe you aren't going to die at the end of it. What you are going through is just the symptoms of a panic attack. As you start seeing them for what they really are then over time they will lessen. You'll also realize that the situation that started the panic attack in the first place wasn't that bad for you after all and the next time you will be able to deal with that situation better the next time you are in it.

I want to make one final point. Even if you do just one of these steps you will start to see some improvements with your depression. However they are designed to work together, they compliment one another well so in the initial stages of getting to grips with your depression try to use them all.

Over time as your depression gets better you can stop using some of the least effective ones. However, these are lifestyle and mindset changes that will take you far beyond your depression.

Beating depression is just part of the battle. To get the very best out of tackling your depression and coping with your every day battles of anxiety, it's important to for you to understand what depression and anxiety is, how it affects you and when and how you should seek treatment.

Suggested Reading

"Beating Depression and Coping With Anxiety".

It shows you:

- Insight into depression so that you can understand what you are going through

- Helps you to understand and identify the symptoms of depression

- The different types of depression so that you can get the right help

- What causes your depression so that you can make the relevant changes

- How you can treat your depression inexpensively

- How you can cope with anxiety and it's symptoms

"The Depression Cure Workbook: The Complete 10 Step Program To Beating Depression."

Here I give you 10 activities for you to:

- Assess your depression and the severity of it

- Identify your strongest emotions so that you can then work on dealing with them

- How to analyze your thoughts and feelings and how they impact on your life

- Learn how to let go of your destructive thoughts and feelings

- **How to change your negative thoughts into positive ones**

- **How to improve your overall social skills to better get on in life**

- **Look and identify areas for change and improvement**

- **Creating plan's for the future**

- **How to create your "Self-Help" plan so that you can take control of your own recovery and your life**

<u>**"The Anxiety Cure Workbook: A Powerful 10 Step Program to Stop Anxiety Now""**</u>

It's has 10 activities for you to complete and <u>you'll find out how to:</u>

- **Measure the severity of your anxious symptoms so that you can start to change them**

- **Help you to deal better with emotional stresses and strains that happen in your everyday life**

- **Help you to better share those feelings and get them out of your system**

- **Acquire new ways to solving your problems**

- **Learn how to assert yourself better and say no to the added pressures in your life**

- **Better manage your conflicts**

- **Learn how to believe in yourself more. If you do others will!**

- **Learn how not to let things worry you so much**

"Take Control Of Your Life: 5 Steps To Maintain A Depression Free Life".

Here you will find ways how to:

- **Keep up with your healthier eating habits and I've included some tasty recipes to help you along the way**

- **Keep up with your exercise regime in order to look and feel great. I've included some fun exercises that you can do**

- **Keep assessing yourself so that you don't go back to your old and destructive ways of dealing with things**

- **How you need to keep up with your journal so that you can see your progress**

- **How to rebuild your life after depression has gone**

www.ingramcontent.com/pod-product-compliance
Lightning Source LLC
Chambersburg PA
CBHW060806290526
45792CB00005BA/1538